This book of poetry is dedicated to every person who has supported me, believed in me, and seen my potential. I was inspired to put this together after doing a forty-day devotion set up by a beautiful friend, a community of women coming together to spur each other on, to be accountable to one another, to share and be open.

Women empowering women, sisterhood, community, friendship all while guiding you to devote time to yourself lovingly and freely.

"An investment in myself became an investment in my art"

Let's Rise Together

Let's rise together
Let's lift each other up
Let's sit with one another
And pour into each other's cup

Let's listen
Let's explore
Let's do what we can
To help each other do more

Let's be patient
Let's be kind
Let's sit in a space
That helps clear our minds

Let's laugh together
Let's cry
No words needed
No what or why

Let's sing together
Let's dance to our own beat
Creating community
In the places we meet

A space to be heard
A space to be seen
A space to be held
A space to just be

A space to connect
A space to be received with love
A space to feel safe
A space to spread your wings like a dove

Let's rise together
Let's lift each other up
Let's sit with one another
And pour into each others cup

To The Women In My Life

Thank you to the women
Who help me to see
That I can be anything
I want to be

Surrounded by women
Inspiring one another
As we realise we aren't alone
And we have each other

Sitting in circles
Knowing we are strong
Finding ourselves
As we see, we do belong

Thank you to my sisters
For holding my hand
As I continue to grow
As my heart expands

Thank you to my Sisters
For your acceptance and love
For your kindness and compassion
For helping me towards conquering my fear of rejection

I love that we see each other
That we hear the said and unsaid
That we are held
And everything is heart-led

Thank you for helping me to feel safe
For the role models you are
For shining light into my life
Just like the moon and stars

Thank you for being real
For the rawness you bring
Feeling the happy and sad
As we let our hearts sing

Strangers to friends
Friends to sisters
Family created
As the love of community hits us

The glue that holds us together
As we find our way home
Walking alongside one another
No one left to walk alone

The Small Details

A cleansing moment
As subtle breeze
Brushes the skin
Bringing a gentle ease

Falling from the top of the head
Through the soles of the feet
Down into the ground
Going deep, deep deep

A relief
A moment to witness
As you lift your head
Slowly landing back with us

A smile beaming just like the sun
As you release and let go
Feeling as light as a feather
Acknowledging how far you have come

The small details
The fine art
Of letting it flow
As you see, it all apart

A gentle moment
A subtle breeze
Now trusting yourself
As you go forward with ease

A Dip in the Sea

As we sit and wait
We already anticipate the cold
But we know the benefits
Of many, we have been told

The fire is built
We embrace the warm
As we sit and chat
And enjoy the calm

It's time to go in
Costumes at the ready
As we walk in
Trying to keep steady

The cold water hits
The coldest it's ever been
But we keep walking in
All shivering yet all keen

We dip down
We take a pause
Proud of each other
All doing it for our own cause

All accepting
All loving
All seen
All hugging

Women empowering women
Embodying all that we are
As we share with each other
And realise we have all come so far

Each of us just human
Navigating our way
On this journey called life
Now set for a new day

Feeling awake, feeling alive
Feeling refreshed and energised
Heart filled with gratitude
For all we have survived

What I Deserve

Sometimes, I have to pinch myself
And ask if this is real
Is this really happening
Is this the real deal

Self-doubt becomes apparent
As I question what I deserve
Thoughts of then and now
Quickly begin to emerge

Taking a step back
As I slowly take a breath
As I prepare myself
For what I allow to happen next

I allow myself a moment
To feel all that wants to come
Before I take a stand
And pick it until it's undone

I talk to myself gently
Reassurance is what I give
As I remind myself
This is my time to live

I deserve the happiness
I deserve all the good that comes
I deserve the moment
I deserve to have fun

I deserve good people
As I learn, I'm someone people want to be around
I don't need to compare
I just need to lift my eyes up from the ground

Lift them up so I can see
That everything is OK
It's time to stop questioning
And start believing what my sisters and brothers say

My sisters and brothers that love me
My sisters and brothers that care
My sisters and brothers, that matter
My sisters and brothers that are there

Feel What You Feel

You need to take time
To sit in the moment
To feel all that it brings
And stop rushing to the next thing

Embrace the comfortable
And the uncomfortable, too
It's in those moments
You can welcome breakthroughs

Nurture the journey you are on
Take it at your own pace
This is lifelong
It is not a race

Connect with others
Have time alone
In the moments of reflection
You will see you have grown

Plant yourself in places
Where you will flourish
As you take steps forward
We celebrate your courage

Root Down

Root down
As you strip it all back
Don't get caught up
On what's the right or wrong track

Root down
As you soften your heart
Take time to look inwards
At every intricate part

Root down
Find your stance
As you focus on what's ahead
Only ever looking back with a glance

Root down
Recognise the courage inside
Keep trusting and believing
And let self-doubt subside

Root down
As you fill your own cup
Take the time you need
You deserve that much

Root down
As you let yourself feel
This is your time
Allow yourself to heal

Time

As the clock ticks
We see the hands move
We feel the urge to rush
To quickly move through

We forget that time is precious
That we should take it in our stride
Live life to the full
With our hearts open wide

Taking in each moment
That the gift of time gives
No longer living to survive
Instead loving the life you live

Grateful for each second
That ticks on by
Taking time to experience joy
Not always having a rhyme or reason why

Time's not on our side
That we each know
So embrace what and who you have
Surrounded by those who help you grow

As time ticks on by
There are always constant shifts
Keep showing up as you are
Don't worry when you drift

Time is a gift
Do with it what you need
And use the opportunities
To plant beautiful new seeds

A time of nurture
A time of embrace
A time of surrender
A time to give grace

I Am

I am woman
I am strong
I am woman
I belong

I am a goddess
A warrior, a queen
I am everything
That's to come, and that's been

I am sister
I am friend
I am me
No need to blend

I am wild
I am free
I am woman
Who can be anything she wants to be

I am courageous
I am bold
I am sensitive
With a heart of gold

I celebrate who I am
I will lift myself up
Surrounded by my sisters
I learn to fill my own cup

I am because I am
And with that, I allow my heart to expand
I am because I am
And with that, I allow myself to land

A Sparkle

A sparkle in your eye
A passion in your heart
A fire ignited
It's never too late to start

As you look around
You see, so much has changed
A transformation is happening
As you're reminded, nothing needs to stay the same

It feels like a dream
Yourself you have to pinch
Every time something good comes
Every time you get a glimpse

It's hard to believe it's real
It's hard to believe it's happening to you
As you thought you deserved unhappiness,
But you know, no that's not true

A life of self-limiting beliefs
It's time to be the change
A life of trauma
It's time to break the chain

You have found love in your heart
You have found joy in your soul
No a day you thought you would see
If the truth be told

You are rising
Feeling empowered from within
A light that glows brightly
That you won't let anyone dim

Stepping out
Knowing it won't always be with ease
But you know you've got this
As you stand strong like the trees

There Are Moments

There are moments
When the old thoughts creep in
A reminder of what once was
A reminder of what's held within

There were always ripples of good
That would be quickly taken away
Because you didn't deserve it
At least that's what they'd say

Moment of terror
Moments of angst
Not knowing what was next
Not knowing if you can or can't

Those fine lines
Instilled deep within
That even now
You sit and wait for it to dim

When things have been good for a while
You start to ask why
Starting to doubt
As time passes by

As time passes by
You sit and worry
Waiting for what's next
Instead of enjoying what is

You expect the worse
You mentally prepare
You begin to create something
That's not even there

You need to break the pattern
You need to believe
That you deserve all this good
One day, I hope that you see

That you see, you are enough
That you see the good you deserve
That you see you are wanted
You're not just a reserve

Be You

Be who you are
Stop expecting the worst
It's in yourself
You need to build that trust

Don't look for outside validation
That must come from within
How you speak to yourself
Is the place to begin

Meet yourself where you are at
Honour wherever that may be
Stop looking for what needs fixed
Give yourself time, you will see

It really is ok
If you are up or down
Allow yourself to feel
Then take some time to ground

Stop the self-sabotage
You're putting out your own flame
It's time to let go
Get rid of all this shame

Manifest Magic

The power of manifestation
The power of trust
The power of believing
They are all a must

When you get out of your way
When you open your heart space
You realise the power within
As you begin to make trace

Trace of your hopes
Trace of your dreams
Trace of seeing things
You never thought you'd see

As you begin to manifest
There's one rule that's a must
Live as if you already have it
As you expand your trust

Feel how having it makes you feel
The smile spread across your face
The joy in your heart
As you give thanks with grace

Align with your higher self
As your vision clears
You will be manifesting magic
Throughout the years

Watch as the magic happens
Watch it all unfold
As you see, your value
Is worth your weight in gold

Manifest with trust
Trust the divine timing
Trust the process
Trust that all is aligning

Reflection

As I stand and stare
Back at my reflection
It raises many questions
On my fear of rejection

I begin to take off the layers
Piece by piece
Right down until
It's my naked self I reach

The divine feminine
I take me all in
My curves and scars
As I slowly begin accepting

Accepting my body
Accepting my story
Accepting my beauty
In all of her glory

Rejection comes from fear
From being in a constant state of compare
But it's time to see the beauty
That is around everywhere

I take one last look
As I feel a peace
Letting go of the lies
The fear I release

Now clothed in acceptance
Clothed in love
Clothed in light
As white as a dove

Loving myself
Every single part
As I give gratitude to my body
For being with me from the start

The Black Sheep

Not quite seen
Not quite heard
Not quite fitting
Not what you deserve

Following the crowd
Blending into the background
Hand across mouth
You don't make a sound

The quiet one
The difficult child
Always in the way
Heads going wild

The black sheep
The one always in the wrong
You hold it all inside
As you try to keep strong

They break you
You say thank you
For that breaking
Has been your making

Your making of escaping
Your making of being strong
Your making to find purpose
Your making to belong

The black sheep always
But no longer stuck
Free from captivity
As you wash away the dirt

Now a vessel
Pulled in by essence
Grateful for those
Who see and feels your presence

You Are Important

I hope you realise
Just how important you are
Your light in this world
Shines as beautiful as the moon and the stars

I hope you know you are seen
Even when you are alone
You are witnessed and celebrated
As you find your way back home

I hope you know you are heard
I hope you know the power your voice holds
That it shakes the earth
When your truth is told

I hope you know you are held
Let yourself melt into our grasp
As we remind you
You are safe at last

I hope you know you matter
And I hope that you see
There is no need to run
Because it's within yourself, you become free

Push against resistance
Push against fear
Push against hesitation
As the mist starts to clear

The journey you are on
Was never to be done alone
Let's straighten your crown
As you reclaim your throne

Balance

Finding the balance
The right amount of control
The right amount of patience
To find calm in your soul

You reach a wall
You feel a bit lost
You're overthinking
Worrying what it's going to cost

The cost of yourself
The cost of friendship
The cost of progress
Doesn't even dent it

You take a deep breath
You try to calm your mind
It's the inner peace
You are trying to find

Not spiralling but evolving
This is just a little twist
A moment of reassurance
As you slowly drift

Pausing for a moment
As you try to catch your thoughts
It's like something within
Has reopened a box

A box of not being wanted
A box of being too much
A box of overthinking
That brings a battle of trust

Just wanting to do good
Wanting to do the best
Sometimes, it feels like
You are stuck in a test

The Power of Letting Go

I watch the trees
As their leaves begin to fall
In awe of how they continue
To stand strong and tall

A reminder of the power
When you release and let go
That it is never the end
There is always room to grow

To grow through the process
To embrace all you are
To stand bare
As you continue to go far

To see the beauty
You need to remove the blinkers
Change the thoughts
That has the power to shrink us

To experience the beauty
Embody the uncomfortable shifts
Then, you will start to see
Things begin to lift

Shower With Intention

As I stand
I set my intention
To let go of it all
Even the stuff I never mention

I turn on the water
I close my eyes
As I look inwards
To where the truth lies

I let go of old patterns
I let go of negative beliefs
I let go of it all
All that's hidden beneath

I welcome in compassion
I welcome in peace
I welcome in positive thoughts
I welcome in new beliefs

I take a moment to remind myself
Of who I am
How far I have come
That I am, and I can

Keep Your Ember Lit

As the flame flickers,
So does our light
Unnoticeable during the day
But obvious at night

We keep it lit
So, focus on what needs done
Forgetting to nurture it
It struggles to burn

Slowly going out
As we forget our self-care
As we forget to take time
We quickly become aware

Aware of our thoughts
Aware of our limits
Aware of our bodies
As we look within us

Giving ourselves a minute
To keep our ember lit
Embracing all that comes
While in a safe place, we sit

We remind ourselves
That it is okay
As we change the narrative
Of what we say

We deserve the light
We deserve the peace
We deserve the love
We deserve the release

Fanning our flame
As it reignites
Giving us hope
That our future is bright

A moment to be still
While in ourselves, we invest
Being the change
With every purposeful breath

A Moment To Be

As the leaves are scattered
Across the ground
We wait with anticipation
Of what will come around

A process of shedding
A process of growth
A process of transformation
Reflecting on all that matters most

The beam of the sun
As it shines on your face
You stand for a moment
Taking in it's warm embrace

You take in its beauty
You listen to birds and the bees
As your heart beats steadily
You feel at ease

Taking in your surroundings
Feeling grateful for it all
Grateful to bear witness
As you watch, the leaves fall

A moment to be
A moment to admire
A moment to feel the magic
As you feel inspired

Allow Yourself A Moment

Allow yourself a moment
To close down your eyes
To take yourself to a place
Where your inner peace lies

Get lost in the moment
As you begin to explore
Feeling each step
As you come to a door

Take a deep breath
As it opens wide
You feel a sense of calm
As you walk on inside

Surrounded by colour
Surrounded by light
As you move around freely
Your passion ignites

You feel a tear
Roll down your face
As you suddenly realise
This is your safe space

A space to get lost
A space to be free
A space to let go
A space to see

To see you matter
To see you belong
To see you have got this
To see you are strong

You open your eyes
With a hand on your heart
Seeing yourself as a whole
No longer in lots of parts

A Prayer For You

I said a prayer for you this morning
As I do every day
Asking the universe
To guide you on your way

That you be surrounded
With whatever you need
Healing and protection
As you take the lead

I ask that you feel her presence
That you feel her in your heart
That you know you aren't alone
Even when you feel so far apart

I ask her to protect you
To shower you with love
That she walks with you
As you await answers from above

I ask her that you know
You have people all around
Who is there for you
Whether you're quiet or making sound

I ask her to be with you
In ways that I can't
I ask her that you hear
Her beautiful chants

I ask her that you know
That I care very much
I am grateful for you
And I am someone you can trust

I ask her that you know
When you rest your head at night
That you are loved beyond measure
Before you turn off the light

Inner Child

Spending time
Trying to connect with my inner child
That I forget other parts of me
That has been closed away for a while

My nineteen-year-old self
The pain in her eyes
The hurt in her heart
Always wanting to die

Six months in a programme
Trying to get better
Only communication outwith
Was in the form of a letter

Full of self-hate
Self-sabotage and self-harm
Wanting to escape
So desperate to find calm

Stuck in destructive patterns
Privileges taken away
Because she didn't know
How to cope another way

My heart aches
As I hold her in my grasp
Finally, letting her know
She is safe at last

No more punishment
No more shame.
Just unconditional love
And a reminder she is brave

I share with her a rose
That was given to me
I let her know I love her
And that we are now free

I Often Wonder

I often wonder
What you would say
If you had been given the chance
The chance to stay

I often wonder what it would be like
To hear your voice
What would we talk about
Would we rejoice

I wonder if you would be proud
I wonder what your guidance would be
Your opinion on things
What we both would see

I wonder if you still know I love you
That I think about you every day
And I often think about seeing you again
And the words I would say

My mind wonders
As I think about you
Trips down memory lane
Often get me through

A Date with My Inner Child

I created a space
Where we both could be
To embrace being safe
To embrace being free

A space to enjoy
A space to connect
A space to relax
A space to accept

To accept ourselves
To accept all is ok
To accept what is and what was
To accept the value in what we say

A space to go inwards
To come to our sacred space
To be like a child
As our memories, we retrace

We enjoy some movies
We enjoy our snacks
We enjoy being together
As we sit back and relax

Creating a bond
As our hearts open
No longer relying on others
To fix what was broken

Holding each other
As we bring an inner peace
As we know that, it's time
For us to finally release

Release all the guilt
Release all the hate
Release all that doesn't serve us
As those thoughts, we replace

A connection with my inner child
I've been too blind to see
That I need her
Just as much as she needs me

Let's Dance

Turning my journey
Into a dance
As I navigate through life
Giving everything a chance

As I dance through the days
My body flows with ease
As I take time to give gratitude
For the moments to be

My rhythm changes
But I go with the beat
It reflects where I am
But I no longer retreat

I dance through the good
I dance through the bad
I dance like no one's watching
The best I ever have

I move through the blockages
I move through the motions
As I finally learn
To invest in self-devotion

Learning to ease up
Learning to breathe
Learning to trust
Learning to believe

Learning not everything is perfect
And that really is ok
We have new opportunities presented to us
Every single day

So, join me in a dance
Wherever that may be
Knowing you aren't alone
As I see you and you can see me

Keep Seeking

We seek but don't often find
We hide, but we don't often seek
We need but don't always ask
We worry we come across weak

We look for validation
We yearn for acceptance
Looking to fit in
Instead of facing rejection

We work on ourselves
We are ready to fly
We experience a joy
Finally feeling alive

During transformation
Clarity arises
Learning to depend on ourselves
No longer hiding behind disguises

Only inward validation
Only seeking from ourselves
Putting ourselves first
For our own sake and our health

Believing we are enough
Realising we do belong
No matter how others treat us
We remain strong

We begin to seek
We begin to find
We begin to trust
As things align

A Human Being

A human being
With thoughts
With feelings
Sometimes just looking
For something to believe in

A human being
Navigating patiently
Not perfect
But moving forward graciously

A human being
A work in progress
A masterpiece forming
Not a one-off project

A human being
No better and no less
Only ever wanting
To do the very best

A human being
Simply grateful to belong
To be seen
In the moments
They struggle to be strong

A human being
That each of us are
Be kind to yourself
And proud of who you are

Stand in your Power

A time to come together
A time to be
A time to connect
A time to see

Time to go inwards
Time to reflect
Time to acknowledge
Areas we might project

A moment to be seen
A moment to be heard
As we share our hearts
Knowing they hear every single word

Surrounded by women
Stepping into our power
Knowing we aren't alone
No matter the hour

We let it come
The laughter, the tears
Knowing we are strong
And can face our fears

As we rise together
We take a stand
As we end the circle
Hand in hand

Thank You, Mama Cacao

As I sit with Mama Cacao
I repeat, mama please
Guide me to where I need to go
Show me what I need to see

Take me to the depths
I try not to go
My heart is open
For what you need to show

Music in the background
My hands guided to my throat
Outcomes sound
Not worrying about hitting notes

A moment of clarity
As everything sounds clear
Magical sound
Echos from ear to ear

A burst of joy
An ecstatic release
As in this moment
It's myself I meet

Vibrations through my body
As Mama cacao flows
Reminding me, I'm safe
I begin to have a subtle glow

Feeling anchored and connected
Giving gratitude for this time
Learning to be present
And not look so far down the line

I raise my voice
As i begin to rise
Realising its within me
That my power lies

Inner Peace

What is peace?
What does it mean to you?
How do you experience it?
How does it get you through?

Peace is a stillness
Like when the water is calm
Peace is internal
When I know, I won't come to harm

Peace is what I see
The nature all around
Taking time to tune in
To every little sound

I experience it in the body
When my heart no longer pounds
When my thoughts slow down
And I can take a moment to be proud

It comes through being creative
As I write, it brings peace
It clears my mind
No thoughts on repeat

Peace comes in all forms.
No right or wrong
Peace takes a moment to remind me
That I do belong

Taking time to go inwards
Taking time to rest
Finding peace in knowing
I am doing my very best

Patience

We are often in a hurry
We want things right away
We want to see the change
We don't want to wait another day

Then we are reminded
Of the gift of time
The gift of patience
Trusting when things will align

We take a moment to pause
We take a moment to trust
A moment to recenter
To calm the rush

Taking a step back
To watch everything flow
Realising we don't need all the answers
We don't always need to know

Practicing patience
Finding our inner peace
As we sit, knowing
Everything will be as it should be

Emotions

Sometimes, it's hard to know
How to feel
How to express
How to be real

How to experience emotions
Such as anger and rage
Knowing you have every reason, too
But they are locked in a cage

Your mind runs wild
A burst of frustration and tears
All internal
So not to upset your fears

You know it's in there
But you don't know how to express
So you sit quietly
Feeling it's a reoccurring test

Emotions pushed down
Not ready to witness
What might come
What might hit us

You are sometimes shaken
You feel the emotions come
But you soothe yourself
So you don't become undone

You put on a smile
You wipe away the tear
Knowing one day
You will break the fear

Choose Yourself Over and Over Again

There came a time when she realised
She had to choose
Because if she doesn't
It's herself she would lose

Would she believe she deserves it
Is she ready to choose breakthrough
Is she ready to do the work
Is she ready to for the big moves

Does she choose to love
Does she choose to chase
Does she choose to fight
Does she choose to embrace

Will she chase the life she wants
Will she chase her hopes and dreams
Will she chase everything
Even the little bits in between

Is she ready let go of worry
To let go of the fears
To let to of the guilt
Carried over the years

Then one day
She finally chose
She chose herself
And daily, she grows

She chooses herself
Over and over again
Learning to be her best friend
Until the very end

Am I Ready?

I step forward
And the question, am I ready?
A slight wobble
I get myself steady

I step forward
With joy in my heart
As I know, each chapter
Is a new place to start

I step forward
With slight hesitation
Worried about the unknown
And all that's left out of the equation

I step forward
Up and ready to go
Ready to fly
Ready to soar

I step forward
My foot firmly in place
As this part of my journey
I'm ready to embrace

The calm
The storm
My heart ignites
As I'm ready to go
As I'm ready to fight

To fight for myself
To fight for all I am
As I stand my ground
While remaining calm

The steps can be scary
But all in your own time
And you will soon see
Things start to fall in line

Permission

Give yourself permission
To do what's right for you
Give yourself permission
To rest or to push through

Listen to your body
To whatever you need
Go for a walk
Or take some time to read

It's ok to pause
To rest and recharge
To take time out
To go watch the moon and stars

It's ok to be busy
To get everything you need done
Just remember to take time
To also have some fun

Give yourself permission
Give yourself time
Give yourself a break
This is your sign

Go barefoot on the grass
Go dance in the rain
Go sing your heart out
Find what lights your flame

Go into hibernation
Go take time for you
Go have those moments of quiet
Go do what's right for you

Give yourself permission
Listen to what you need
You have got this
It's up to you to take the lead

Invest In You

As I took time
To invest in me
I went outside
To be at one with the trees

As I took time
To invest in me
I went to the water
As she makes me feel at ease

As I took time
To invest in me
I got creative
And wrote poetry

To invest in me
Was to create a space
Where I could go inwards
And feel safe

A daily devotion
To open my heart
To witness myself
To see every single part

Honouring all of me
As I say, thanks
For this opportunity
For this beautiful chance

The chance to learn
The chance to connect
The chance to grow
The chance to welcome what's next

Daily Devotion

Time to devote
Time to care
Time to be
Time to share

What a beautiful reminder
To put yourself first
To take the time you need
In the process, you trust

Daily devotion
Whatever that may be
That time to go inwards
Can help set you free

Not a routine
Not a chore
But a daily practice
To help you grow more

Give yourself the time
That you truly deserve
And even when you are alone
Know you are heard

So carve out that time
To invest in you
Because you deserve it
And it will see you through

You've Got This

You didn't think you could do it
But you kept going
You showed up for you
Sometimes, without even knowing

You allowed vulnerability
You allowed yourself to feel
You allowed the darkness
In order to heal

If you haven't already
Know you're going to make it through
This is your time
So be all in for you

Through it all
Remember, you aren't alone
Surrounded by many that love you
Who will support you in growing

Take time alone
Take time to connect
With an open heart
Ready for what's next

Acknowledgement

Thank you for taking the time to invest and read my work; it is appreciated.

I have had a love for writing from a young age; it's been my way to express myself and has been my voice for such a long time, which makes it even more beautiful to take this step and share it with you all.

I have so much gratitude for each person who has encouraged me to take this step and who has taken the time to read.

My encouragement to you would be that whatever you are holding on to and hoping to achieve – go for it; there is no better time than now.

You can find more of my work on –
Instagram - @lifethroughwordsmb
Facebook – Life Through Words

Printed in Great Britain
by Amazon

41059922R00024